FEEL, THINK AND DO
WITH RUBY, RAFA AND RIZ

This children's storybook tells the story of Ruby, Rafa and Riz as each child has an experience that affects them – unkind friendship, the death of a pet, a bullying family member and coercive peers. Their teacher, who knows nothing of these events, notices the behaviour of each child which leads to him asking how they are feeling and what they are thinking, enabling each child to talk about their emotions and so helping the adult to understand their behaviour.

In a clever and enjoyable way, the stories of Ruby, Rafa and Riz lead children through scenarios that introduce ideas key to developing children's understanding and security such as the:

- knowledge that behaviour is a response to feelings and thoughts

- understanding that these feelings and thoughts are a response to the external world

- insight into how thoughts and feelings are hidden unless shared; and the

- empowerment to share their emotional context with trusted adults, explaining their behaviour – both to others and themselves.

When used alongside the practical guidebook, this unique and engaging story enables all those working directly with children to support their development, allowing children to become strong enough and secure enough to meet the challenges of life and learning.

Liz Bates is an independent education consultant. She supports both primary and secondary schools in all aspects of Emotional Health and Wellbeing, and Safeguarding, including whole school approaches, training staff and delivering talks to parents. Liz is a Protective Behaviours Trainer, a Wellbeing Award Advisor for Optimus and a regular contributor at national conferences.

Feel, Think and Do with Ruby, Rafa and Riz:

Understanding Behaviour and Emotions

Liz Bates

Illustrated by Nigel Dodds

Routledge
Taylor & Francis Group

LONDON AND NEW YORK

Cover image © Nigel Dodds

First published 2022
by Routledge
2 Park Square, Milton Park, Abingdon, Oxon OX14 4RN

and by Routledge
605 Third Avenue, New York, NY 10158

Routledge is an imprint of the Taylor & Francis Group, an informa business

British Library Cataloguing-in-Publication Data
A catalogue record for this book is available from the British Library

Library of Congress Cataloging-in-Publication Data
Names: Bates, Liz, author. | Dodds, Nigel (Archaeological illustrator), illustrator.
Title: Ruby, Rafa and Riz : understanding behaviour and emotions / Liz Bates ;
    illustrated by Nigel Dodds.
Description: Abingdon, Oxon ; New York, NY : Routledge, 2022. | Audience: Grades K-1 |
Identifiers: LCCN 2021037581 (print) | LCCN 2021037582 (ebook) | ISBN 9781032059433
    (paperback) | ISBN 9781003199960 (ebook)
Subjects: LCSH: Emotions in children--Juvenile literature. | Child psychology--Juvenile
    literature.
Classification: LCC BF723.E6 B38 2022 (print) | LCC BF723.E6 (ebook) |
    DDC 155.4/124--dc23/eng/20211115
LC record available at https://lccn.loc.gov/2021037581
LC ebook record available at https://lccn.loc.gov/2021037582

ISBN: 978-1-032-05943-3 (pbk)
ISBN: 978-1-003-19996-0 (ebk)

DOI: 10.4324/9781003199960

Typeset in Apple Casual
by Deanta Global Publishing Services Chennai India

Ruby, Rafa and Riz are just like you.

They live with their families.

Ruby has 2 brothers and 2 sisters.

Rafa lives with his foster mum.

Riz has lots of cousins.

Ruby, Rafa and Riz are all in the same class at school.

Mr Potter is their class teacher.

1

Ruby likes running and riding her bike but doesn't like pizza or the sound of thunder.

Rafa likes sausages and his local football team but doesn't like cricket or the smell of his brother's aftershave.

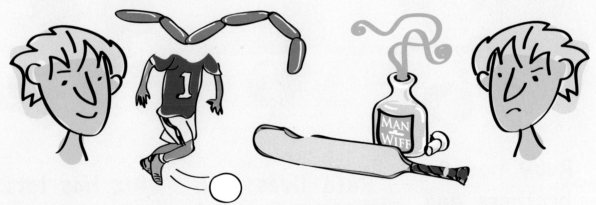

Riz likes video games and playing with his cousins but doesn't like breakfast cereal or having to sit still.

When everyone has to sing in assembly, Ruby is really happy but Rafa is fed up.

When Rafa's favourite football team wins, Rafa is really pleased but Riz doesn't care.

When sports day is cancelled because of the rain, Riz is relieved but Ruby is disappointed.

Have you noticed that Ruby, Rafa and Riz feel differently about the same thing? Are you like that too?

Ruby is friends with Meera, Lulu and Milly. They have known each other since their first day at school.

Ruby has invited her friends to a sleepover on Friday night. She is very excited and hopes they will have lots of fun.

At breaktime on Friday, Ruby says her favourite boy band is different to the one her friends like. There is lots of whispering and giggling from the 3 girls and Ruby is left out.

No one comes to Ruby's sleepover and nobody answers Ruby's messages over the weekend.

Ruby has lots of feelings going on inside of her. She has lots of thoughts going on inside her head.

Ruby doesn't know where all these feelings and thoughts are coming from and she doesn't know what to do with them.

How might Ruby be feeling?

What might Ruby be thinking?

What might Ruby do?

Ruby feels like she has no friends.
Is this true?
She thinks everyone hates her.
Do they?

Ruby wants to be mean to everyone.
Is this her only choice?

At school on Monday Ruby bangs her chair, doesn't talk to anyone, doesn't put her hand up to answer any questions and rips up Lulu's worksheet. This isn't like Ruby.

Mr Potter doesn't know what is wrong. He doesn't understand why Ruby would do those things. He thinks Ruby must be in a bad mood.

It's Tuesday morning and Rafa doesn't want to go to school. Rafa's dog Buster has been poorly and last night he and mum took Buster to the vet.

The vet said Buster was too poorly to go back home.

Rafa is very sad and he feels sick this morning. Rafa doesn't want to go to school but his mum gets cross and says he has to go.

They are so late for school that his mum doesn't have time to write a note to explain to Mr Potter about Buster.

At school Rafa has lots of feelings going on inside of him.

He has lots of thoughts going on inside his head.

Rafa doesn't know where all these feelings and thoughts are coming from and he doesn't know what to do with them.

How might Rafa be feeling?

What might Rafa be thinking?

What might Rafa do?

Rafa feels like he wants to cry.
Is it ok for him to do that?
Rafa thinks his best friend Billy will tease him if he cries.
Do friends do that?
Rafa wants to shout at someone and break something.
Is this Rafa's only choice?

At breaktime Rafa shouts at his best friend Billy, kicks Billy's football over the fence and then sits on his own.

Billy is really puzzled. Usually he and Rafa have fun together.

Mr Potter doesn't know what is wrong. He doesn't understand why Rafa would do those things. Is Rafa in a bad mood too?

It's Wednesday morning and Riz's uncle has been teasing him again. Uncle Mo teases Riz for not being in the football team and Riz wishes his mum would make him stop.

Riz doesn't always enjoy school. He is sometimes called names when he gets things wrong.

Riz has lots of feelings going on inside of him.

He has lots of thoughts going on inside his head.

Riz doesn't know where all these feelings and thoughts are coming from and he doesn't know what to do with them.

At breaktime on Wednesday some of the boys in Riz's class tell him that if he hides Leon's PE kit, they will let him play with them at lunchtime. Riz likes the sound of that as he is often on his own at lunchtime.

How might Riz be feeling?

What might Riz be thinking?

What might Riz do?

Riz feels he doesn't want to spend lunchtime alone.

He thinks the boys will like him if he does what they say.

He wants to get back at his uncle and everyone else.

At the end of breaktime Riz puts Leon's PE kit in the bin, pours some water over it and won't say sorry.

Mr Potter doesn't know what is wrong. He doesn't understand why Riz would do that.

Is everyone in a bad mood this week?

Is there anything that Ruby, Rafa and Riz can do to help Mr Potter understand why they did those things?

Mr Potter sits down with Ruby.

"How are you today Ruby? I think you might be feeling angry. Can I help you? Is there anything you can tell me to help me understand why you tore up Lulu's work?
Can you tell me how you were feeling and what you were thinking?"

Ruby tells him how she was feeling and what she was thinking.

Now Mr Potter understands why Ruby did what she did.

Mr Potter has lunch with Rafa.

"How are you today Rafa? I think you might be feeling upset. Can I help you? Is there anything you can tell me to help me understand why you fell out with Billy? Can you tell me what you were feeling and thinking this morning?"

Rafa tells him how he was feeling and what he was thinking.

Now Mr Potter understands why Rafa did what he did.

Mr Potter walks round the playground with Riz.

"How are you today Riz? I think you might be feeling unhappy. Can I help you? Is there anything you can tell me to help me understand why you spoiled Leon's kit? What feelings and thoughts did you have?"

Riz tells him how he was feeling and what he was thinking.

Now Mr Potter understands why Riz did what he did.

Mr Potter knows how important it is to talk about your feelings and thoughts and how these can affect your behaviour.

He decides everyone in the class should know about the imaginary iceberg.

26

Ruby, Rafa and Riz agree.
And now it's your turn to learn
about the imaginary iceberg.